THE LIBRARY OF
AMERICAN
LIVES AND TIMES™

DOLLEY MADISON

Her Life, Letters, and Legacy

Holly C. Shulman
David B. Mattern

The Rosen Publishing Group's
PowerPlus Books™
New York

For Rebecca, Jonathan, Pauline, and Benjamin

Published in 2003 by The Rosen Publishing Group, Inc.
29 East 21st Street, New York, NY 10010

First Edition

Editor's Note: All quotations have been reproduced as they appeared in the letters and diaries from which they were borrowed. No correction was made to the inconsistent spelling that was common in that time period.

Library of Congress Cataloging-in-Publication Data

Shulman, Holly Cowan.
Dolley Madison : her life, letters, and legacy / Holly C. Shulman and David B. Mattern.
    p. cm. — (The library of American lives and times)
Summary: Surveys the life of First Lady Dolley Madison, wife of the fourth president, who was renowned as a hostess, a lady of fashion, and a heroine of the War of 1812.
Includes bibliographical references and index.
  ISBN 0-8239-5749-7 (lib. bdg.)
1. Madison, Dolley, 1768–1849—Juvenile literature. 2. Presidents' spouses—United States—Biography—Juvenile literature. [1. Madison, Dolley, 1768–1849. 2. First ladies. 3. Women—Biography.] I. Mattern, David B., 1951– II. Title. III. Series.
  E342.1 .S47 2003
  973.5'1'092—dc21

                                                    2002007052

Manufactured in the United States of America

CONTENTS

Introduction

On September 4, 1886, an important publishing house printed a collection of Dolley Madison's letters, called *Memoirs and Letters of Dolly Madison*. The letters had been collected by Dolley's grandniece, Lucia B. Cutts. The book went through several printings over the next twenty-nine years, until the last edition came out in 1915. It was the beginning of a series of biographies of Dolley Madison, whose name is often misspelled "Dolly," as more and more Americans wanted to know about this famous American first lady who had been the first to preside over Washington, D.C., and was known as the heroine of the War of 1812.

By the beginning of the twentieth century, Dolley was beginning to be remembered in other ways. A cake company took the name Dolly Madison Cakes for the famous hostess. A women's shoe company in Virginia used the

---

Opposite: While he was secretary of state, James Madison commissioned this 1804 portrait of Dolley by Gilbert Stuart. This portrait is the best-known likeness of Dolley Madison. It hangs in the White House on the west wall of the Red Room, which during Dolley's time was the Yellow Drawing Room where Dolley held her receptions as first lady.

name to recall the famous American woman of fashion. A wine company named a wine for her in 1934, to tell Americans that drinking wine is a gesture of hospitality that has a respectable past in the United States.

Today many highways and hotels are named for her. In 1980, the U.S. government issued a stamp in her honor. Over the course of the twentieth century, there have not only been Dolley Madison cakes and shoes, but Dolley Madison suitcases and hats, popcorn and ice cream, and coins and Christmas decorations. No other woman in American history has been so honored and remembered.

Who was this woman? Where was she born? How did she grow up? Most of all, what made her so famous and important?

1. "Bright Dawn of a New Day"

Dolley Madison's parents were Quakers named John Payne and Mary Coles Payne. Both John and Mary grew up on rural, eastern-Virginia plantations. They were married in 1761, and settled on land owned by the Payne family. The couple took their religion seriously, but perhaps they also wanted adventure. In 1765, they left their families and friends and moved to North Carolina in the company of other members of the Society of Friends. In the remoteness of the wilderness, they planned to dedicate themselves to religious discipline. Such a life was hard from the very beginning. Even the journey was difficult. The route often wound through narrow forest paths. Sometimes trees and boulders blocked their way. They had to climb across mountains, all the while being careful to avoid bears, rattlesnakes, and other wildlife.

The Paynes settled in the middle of North Carolina. They were some of the first white people to live near what today is the town of Guilford. Now the homestead is located on the busy road between Greensboro and

Quakers are a Christian group also known as the Society of Friends. They reject ritual and an ordained ministry and they oppose war. In the eighteenth century, they often lived in their own communities in order to worship together. They believe in living a simple, moral life. They call their churches meetinghouses.

Winston-Salem. In those days, it was an isolated community called New Garden, clustered around a Quaker meetinghouse.

Dolley Madison was born Dolley Payne on May 20, 1768. She was the third child born to John and Mary Coles Payne to survive infancy. She had two older brothers, named Walter and William Temple. Soon Isaac would also join the Payne family.

After four years in North Carolina, John and Mary Payne returned to Virginia. They left behind no explanation for this decision. We do know that few Quakers who moved from Virginia to North Carolina returned home.

The Paynes must have found their new life either unsatisfactory or too difficult. Maybe their decision to go home was the result of personal needs. Perhaps it was a consequence of the political and economic conditions of that time in North Carolina. By the 1760s, North Carolina was beginning to seethe with unrest. Farmers within North Carolina joined together to oppose taxes that they declared were too high. Newer settlers in western North Carolina rallied to proclaim that easterners had too much power. Anger swelled, and the protest movement grew. Perhaps the Payne family simply chose to move as a way out of the conflict.

In 1769, they returned to Virginia and settled down in Hanover County. There they had at least four more children. This time there were three girls, named Lucy, Anna, and Mary, and one more boy, John Coles. There may have been others who died in infancy, a sad but common fact of life during this time.

Virginia was the oldest, the biggest, and the most populous British colony in North America. Its economy was dominated by tobacco, although by the 1770s, farmers were also beginning to grow grain, especially wheat, to sell. During the 1760s, Virginia did not experience the kind of unrest that plagued North Carolina.

Next page: Hanover County is circled in pink on this 1781 map created by aide-de-camp Michel du Chesnoy for Marquis de Lafayette during the American Revolution. The map shows central Virginia, including bridges, houses, churches, taverns, and other points of interest.

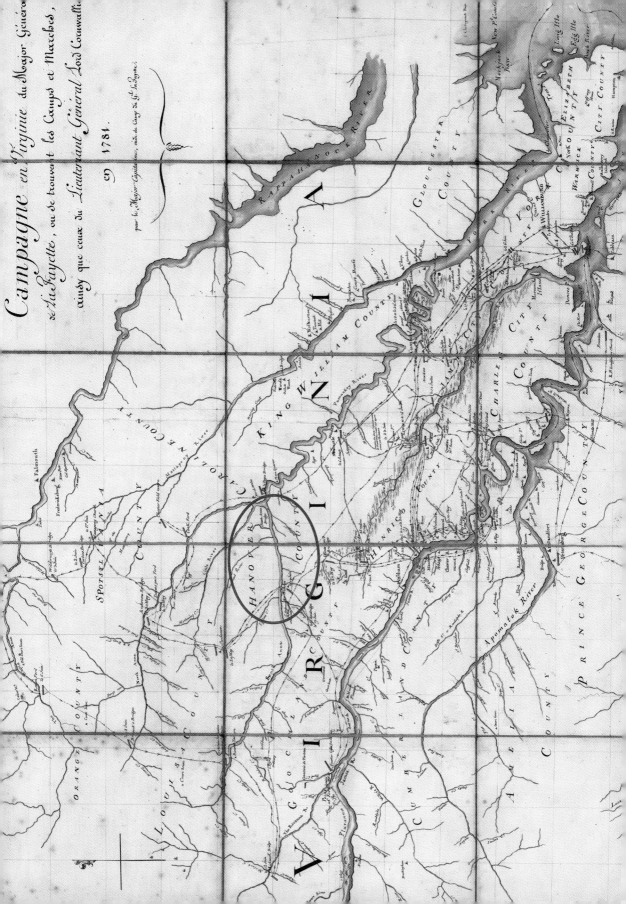

Scotchtown was built around 1719, by Charles Chiswell.
It is one of the oldest surviving plantation houses in Virginia.
Patrick Henry and his family lived there from 1771 to 1778.

There are many conflicting stories about where the Paynes lived upon their return to Virginia. Many people say that they rented Scotchtown Plantation. It is believed that this story mainly exists to highlight Dolley's relation to Patrick Henry, a prominent figure in Virginia society and the owner of Scotchtown. However, there is no proof that the Payne family ever stayed there. It is more likely that, for financial reasons, the Paynes had to move in with the family of Dolley's mother at Coles Hill Plantation.

Nevertheless, the violence from which they had fled in North Carolina caught up with them in Virginia a decade later. In the 1770s, Virginia became a leader in the anti-British activities that followed the French and Indian War (1754–1763). Protests against taxes imposed by the British government through acts such as the Stamp Act of 1765 and the Townshend Acts of 1767 became common in Virginia and throughout the colonies. Virginia's leaders held meetings and formed committees for self government, while men like Patrick Henry urged Virginians and Americans to take up arms and to seize their independence. All of these things led to the outbreak of the American Revolution on April 19, 1775.

Patrick Henry's famous, fiery speeches helped inspire Americans to seize their independence. David Silvette's portrait of Henry, above, is based on Thomas Sully's portrait, which was painted after Henry's death.

Thus, the Paynes found themselves in the middle of a war. The conflict raging around them was not just a rebellion against England, however. It was a three-sided struggle. There was a war against the Native Americans, who were angry that the colonists had stolen native land. There was a war against Britain,

The American Revolution began with the Battle of Lexington and Concord. Amos Doolittle created the above engraving of the battle scene at Lexington based on eyewitness accounts. He made four different engravings documenting the battles fought on April 19, 1775, at both Lexington and Concord.

who wanted to keep control over its colonies. There was a war against the Tories, neighbors who were loyal to Great Britain and who did not want Virginia to become independent. For Quakers, who were forbidden by their religion to support war in any way, it was a very difficult period. Many patriots assumed Quakers were loyal to the George III, king of England, because they would not fight.

It was especially hard for Dolley's father. He did not believe in war, and he did not believe in slavery. These

George III, king of England (1738-1820), in an undated illustration, became the focus for much of the resentment in the colonies during the American Revolution.

were two things that were hard to get away from at this time in Virginia. Dolley's father took his Quaker faith quite seriously. John Payne believed if you were a good Quaker, then you could not support slavery. As one Quaker preacher proclaimed, "the life of religion is almost lost where slaves are numerous, the practice being as contrary to the spirit of Christianity as light is to darkness." The Paynes, however, had inherited slaves from their families, and they were not allowed to free them, by Virginia's law. Finally in 1782, Virginians passed laws to allow slave owners to free their slaves. Dolley's father now had the opportunity to manumit, or free, his slaves and to unshackle his conscience. He did so.

That meant another move. The family could not support themselves on a Virginian farm without slave labor. Even if they had wanted to stay, there was a lot of

By 1750, there were about 200,000 enslaved blacks in the colonies. By the early 1800s, more than 700,000 slaves worked on southern plantations. In this 1798 watercolor by Benjamin Henry Latrobe, slaves are shown working in a field supervised by an overseer.

hostility from other planters to anyone, Quaker or not, who freed their slaves. Moreover, the Paynes wanted to live where slavery had been abolished. In 1783, when Dolley was fifteen years old, her parents moved to Philadelphia to create a new life for the family.

They already knew a few people in this Quaker metropolis known as the City of Brotherly Love. They found a house, and Dolley's father decided to set up shop as a small merchant, this time in the laundry starch business. The family settled in.

The Paynes moved to Philadelphia, Pennsylvania, around 1783. Above is a view of the city and the bustling port of Philadelphia from 1800. This painting, *The City and Port of Philadelphia on the River Delaware from Kensington*, was created by William Russell Birch and his son Thomas.

Philadelphia was an exciting place to live. It was the largest city in the new nation. It was the leading commercial center. It was noisy and rich. Small shops dotted the city where the streets were paved with brick and were shaded by rows of buttonwood, willow, and poplar trees. The houses of the very wealthy were modeled on London mansions with soaring staircases, French wallpaper, and chairs upholstered in silk.

From the beginning, Dolley Payne shone. She loved the largeness of the city and wanted a merry life. Her family joined the Pine Street Meeting, which was often crowded and was filled with cheerful young people. As Anthony Morris, one of her early friends there, recalled years later, her entrance was the "bright dawn of a new day." She was lovely as she moved through the world with her "stately step, and the sweet engaging Smile."

In the late 1780s, however, her father's business failed. The Pine Street Meeting expelled him for debt. Dolley's mother turned their residence into a boardinghouse, while John Payne became extremely depressed. He retreated into his bedroom and rarely came out until he died on October 24, 1792.

Charles Willson Peale painted this portrait of Anthony Morris around 1789. Morris lived from 1766 to 1860. He was the director of the Bank of North America between 1800 and 1806.

2. "Dying on our right hand and on our left"

In 1789, Dolley Payne became engaged to marry John Todd Jr., a young Quaker lawyer who had courted her for years. He was an up-and-coming young attorney with a good future ahead of him. Another man might have broken his engagement after his fiancée's father failed in business. The Payne family had been publicly humiliated. Dolley was lovely and charming, however. Throughout her father's decline, John Todd stood by her, and in the end she agreed to marry him. In late 1789, John Todd and Dolley Payne asked permission from the Pine Street Meeting to be united, and on January 7, 1790, they wed.

There were two marriages that day at the meeting-house, and the building was very crowded. At the appointed time, Dolley Payne and John Todd stood up in front of the congregation, just the two of them, there for all to see. Each repeated the marriage vows, and then each signed the marriage certificate. After they were done, friends crowded around them to sign the document and to bear witness to their union. Dolley's parents and

Dolley Payne and John Todd were married
at the Pine Street Meeting, pictured above
in a photograph from 1859.

John Todd is shown here in a miniature on ivory painted sometime between 1830 and 1840. John Todd was born around 1760 and died from yellow fever in 1793.

her sisters joined the crush, along with John Todd's brother and sister-in-law, James and Alice Todd. Dolley's friend, Eliza Collins, who would be at Dolley Madison's bedside when she died nearly sixty years later, was there too. Anthony Morris, who would also remain her friend throughout their lives, also attended her marriage to John Todd.

The Todds soon moved into a house on South Fourth Street in Philadelphia. At about the same time, the U.S. government moved from New York City to Philadelphia. The city became even livelier as people flocked there from all of the thirteen states.

In their new house, John Todd carried on his law practice, walking from his upstairs bedroom to his first-floor office to start the day's business. John Todd had two young men apprenticed to him to study law. These men also lived in the Todd house. When Dolley or John

Todd looked out of their windows, they could see the home of Benjamin Rush, one of the city's leading physicians. Another neighbor, William White, was one of the wealthiest men in the new nation. White was a very important figure in Philadelphia and a friend of President George Washington. He was bishop of the Episcopal Church of America and chaplain of the U.S. Senate. White spent time socializing with the nation's leaders, including John Adams and Thomas Jefferson.

The members of the new government were not part of the Todds' life, however. The Todd house was not grand. There were only six rooms, two on each of three floors. Their circle of acquaintances remained largely Quaker.

The federal government in 1790 was tiny when compared to that of today. It consisted of three branches, as it does today. The executive branch was made up of the president, the vice president, their private secretaries, the attorney general, the postmaster general, their clerks, and the secretaries of state, war, the treasury, and the navy. The legislative branch consisted of 65 members of the House of Representatives and 26 members of the Senate, the secretary of the Senate, the clerk of the House, two doorkeepers, and the sergeant at arms of the House. Six justices of the Supreme Court made up the judicial branch.

Benjamin Rush, shown here in an undated portrait based on one by Charles Willson Peale, was very involved in politics and was a prominent doctor in Philadelphia. He was also a signer of the Declaration of Independence.

The Todds were neither rich nor poor. Their life was comfortable. Dolley Todd did her own housework and cooking. She purchased her fish, meat, fruit, and bread from nearby merchants, to feed her family and her husband's law clerks. She also ran the house and managed the apprentices when her husband was away.

In the first few years after she was married and moved away from home, she worried about her mother, who was still running a boardinghouse. Then in 1792, her younger sister Lucy eloped with George Washington's nephew George Steptoe Washington. Mary Coles Payne sold her boardinghouse, bundled up her belongings and her two youngest children, and set off to live with Lucy. They lived at Harewood, a Washington family plantation in western Virginia, in comfort and security.

Dolley Todd's first child, John Payne Todd, was born in February 1792. Her second son, William Temple Todd, was born early in the summer of 1793. The couple loved their two young boys. When John Todd traveled for his law practice, he made sure he wrote home and sent his love. "I hope my dear Dolley is well," he penned in July 1793, "& my sweet Payne can lisp Mama in a stronger Voice than when his Papa left him." He wished his oldest son was there in the countryside with him, to play with the farm animals and to run around.

Three months later, disaster struck. In August 1793, a deadly yellow fever epidemic engulfed Philadelphia.

George Davis Ejus Liber
Bt. 1803
Price $1=25

AN

ACCOUNT

OF THE

Bilious remitting Yellow Fever,

A S

IT APPEARED

IN THE

CITY OF PHILADELPHIA,

IN THE YEAR 1793.

By Benjamin Rush, M.D.

PROFESSOR OF THE INSTITUTES, AND OF CLINICAL MEDICINE,
IN THE UNIVERSITY OF PENNSYLVANIA.

PHILADELPHIA,
PRINTED BY THOMAS DOBSON,
AT THE STONE-HOUSE, Nº 41, SOUTH SECOND-STREET.

MDCCXCIV.

M.E.W.

Benjamin Rush was known as the leading expert of his time in treating epidemics. He wrote *An Account of the Bilious remitting Yellow Fever, as It Appeared in the City of Philadelphia, in the Year 1793,* which was printed by Thomas Dobson. Leaders from around the world consulted him on the treatment of this deadly disease.

It lasted for months. Fear ran rampant. In the eighteenth century, no one understood why the disease occurred, how to prevent it, or how to cure it. Husbands abandoned their wives, and wives left their husbands. Children were orphaned, and whole families were wiped out. The city's doctors proposed varying and contradictory remedies, and ordinary citizens resorted to a host of useless measures. They fired muskets, they chewed tobacco, they burned bonfires, they rang bells, they smoked bedding with tobacco, and they carried pieces of rope covered with tar. All of these actions were taken, of course, to no avail. Panic radiated up and down the Atlantic coast, and New York and New Jersey passed laws forbidding people from Philadelphia to enter their states.

In the midst of all this, John Todd sent his wife and two young sons off to the country. He stayed in town. He had business to do. The need for lawyers to settle estates and to conduct ordinary business steadily expanded as the plague took a greater toll on the city's citizens. The situation grew ever more frightening. In mid-September, one of John Todd's apprentices, a young man named Isaac Heston, wrote a letter to his brother. "You cannot imagine the situation of this city," he declared. "They are dying on our right hand and on our left. Great are the number that are called to the grave, and numbered with the silent dead."

By the time the epidemic ended, about five thousand people had perished. Dolley's husband John Todd passed away on October 14, 1793. Dolley's baby son, William Temple, died a few days later. Two more lives had been claimed by the yellow fever epidemic.

Dolley Payne Todd had lost three of her brothers, her father, her parents-in-law, her baby boy, and her husband all in a few years. Her sense of loss and anxiety never left her.

3. "In this union"

On a May morning in 1794, the young widow Dolley Todd rushed to her writing desk and hurriedly scrawled a note to her best friend, Eliza Collins Lee: "Thou must come to me. Aaron Burr says that the great little Madison has asked to be brought to see me this evening."

James Madison probably would have been surprised, but secretly delighted, to find that he had caused Dolley such excitement. He was a forty-three-year-old bachelor and the son of a Virginia plantation owner. James Madison had made a great name for himself as a politician. Despite the fact that he was a slight and shy man who avoided the public spotlight, Madison had

Eliza Collins Lee is shown here in a portrait by Alice Matilda Reading, painted between 1879 and 1934.

been an important delegate to the Continental Congress during the American Revolution. James Madison had played a major role in the 1787 Constitutional Convention. He also had a large impact on the first federal congresses after 1789, especially through his work drafting the Bill of Rights. James Madison was a well-known figure in Philadelphia and in the new nation.

The Virginian, however, was not Dolley Todd's sole suitor. A number of men were attracted to her youth,

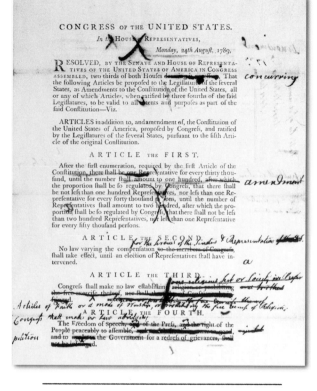

Madison gave a speech about the Bill of Rights at the First Federal Congress on June 8, 1789. The men attending the Congress worked hard to create a document that would protect the individual rights of the people, as can be seen in all the handwritten changes on this draft of the bill.

her beauty, and her property. In fact, an old friend some years later described her as raising the mercury "in the

Opposite: James Madison is shown in a gold-cased miniature portrait painted by Charles Willson Peale in 1783. The portrait was given to Catherine "Kitty" Floyd, presented as a pin in a velvet case. Madison had been engaged to Kitty when he was 31 and she was 15, but she chose to marry another man.

Dolley's engagement ring is pictured above. It was made of yellow and rose gold and set with diamonds. Dolley's grandniece said, "this ring Mrs. Madison wore always & died with it upon her hand."

thermometers of the Heart to fever heat." With so many possibilities, Dolley Todd spent the summer thinking about her future life. By the end of August, she had agreed to marry James Madison.

They were wed at Harewood, the estate where Dolley's sister Lucy lived with her husband, George Steptoe Washington. The ceremony took place on September 15, 1794. It was a quiet affair, as most marriages were at this time, with only the immediate families attending. After a year of horrible loss, Dolley Madison found security in her new marriage. As she wrote that day to Eliza Collins Lee, "In this union I have every thing that is soothing and grateful in prospect—and my little Payne will have a generous and tender protector." So began forty-two years of loving partnership.

As the wife of James Madison, Dolley led a life much different from any she had ever known. She was expelled from the Pine Street Meeting after she married the slave-holding, non-Quaker Madison. With that

This is the parlor at Harewood in which Dolley Payne Todd and James Madison were married on September 15, 1794.

event, she left her plain style of living behind. The Madisons moved into a large, fashionable brick house on cobblestone-paved Spruce Street. They purchased new furnishings. By the end of their stay in Philadelphia, they had filled their house with French sofas and chairs, glassware, and elegant silverware and candlesticks. They attended plays, went to balls, made visits, and shared gossip. As a congressman, James was invited everywhere, and Dolley took to her new lifestyle with zest.

This is a room in the house at 429 Spruce Street, in which the Madisons lived when they moved to Philadelphia. Now called Stride-Madison House, the house is part of the Historic American Buildings Survey held at the Library of Congress in Washington, D.C.

Their days in Philadelphia came to an end in the spring of 1797, when James Madison decided not to run again for Congress. Political warfare between the Federalist Party and his own Republican Party had grown bitter. Each side saw the other, not as rival politicians, but as traitors. Each side believed their opponents wanted to overthrow the ideals of the American Revolution. Besides, James Madison had been in Congress for almost eight years. It was time to retire.

This silk needlework and watercolor, from around 1825 to 1838, of Montpelier by Frances Emeline Husted shows what Montpelier looked like when James and Dolley Madison retired there in 1817.

They left the big city for rural Virginia. Montpelier, the Madison family estate, was located in Orange County in the Piedmont, the region at the foot of the Blue Ridge Mountains. There James Madison and his father supervised a plantation of more than 5,000 acres (2,023 ha). Wealthy southern plantation owners, or planters, as they were known, used slaves to cultivate their vast farms. The Madisons owned more than one hundred slaves. Among them were skilled artisans and laborers, including blacksmiths, carpenters, wheelwrights, spinners, and

weavers. Slaves planted tobacco, corn, and wheat and raised cattle, hogs, and sheep. They also did the house-work. The plantation bustled with activity, depending on the season.

The Madisons' house sat on a knoll with a breath-taking view of the Blue Ridge Mountains, which were 20 miles (32 km) away. It was a large, two-story brick building with a central hallway and rooms on each side. In their first years back home, the Madisons added more rooms so that everyone could have privacy. On one side lived James Madison's parents. On the other side lived James, Dolley, her son John Payne Todd, and Dolley's sister Anna Payne.

Family and friends took on added importance in the isolated Virginia countryside. The Madisons traveled around the state to other plantations for visits that could last as long as one or two weeks. They rode to neighboring farms for parties, dinners, and barbecues and even went to Richmond for the meeting of the Virginia General Assembly. When they were not travel-ing, Montpelier was, as Dolley once wrote, always "full of company, relations, connections, neighbors, and strangers." One letter Dolley wrote from Monticello, when the Madisons were visiting Thomas Jefferson in

Opposite: This map was made from surveys done before the American Revolution. It was published by Robert Sayer and John Bennett in 1776. Orange County, Virginia, where Montpelier is located, is circled in blue.

1797, shows how busy she could be. "We left Mr. Madison's sisters on their Annual visit to us, and we expect my Mother and sisters have joined them some days since—we are therefore oblidged to hasten back."

In 1801, however, two events intervened to bring this gay and carefree life to a temporary halt. James Madison's father died in February, and Thomas Jefferson took office as third president of the United States.

The first meant that James Madison would inherit Montpelier, with all its wealth and responsibilities. Dolley Madison would become its mistress, with great responsibilities of her own.

The second event meant that the Madisons would be called to live in the new capital city of Washington, D.C. Their old friend Thomas Jefferson had asked James Madison to be secretary of state. Once again, Dolley Madison was beginning a new life.

4. "In social circles all are equal"

When the Madisons arrived in Washington, the capital was a village of about three thousand people, most of whom lived in badly built wooden houses. These homes were spread here and there along the roughly cleared streets. There were also some substantial brick homes scattered about. The President's House, which became known as the White House much later, dominated its stretch of Pennsylvania Avenue, much as the Capitol did its hill. The streets, however, were knee deep in mud or dust, depending on the weather, and were filled with potholes and tree stumps. It was a far cry from the elegant and populous capital it would become.

Dolley and James eventually settled in a three-story brick house on F Street, two blocks from the President's House. Their house included cellars to store wine and coal and a stable out back for a carriage and horses. There was enough space for the Madison family, which included Payne Todd and Anna Payne, as well as room for large dinners and parties, of which there were many.

Benjamin Henry Latrobe, an architect, painted this view of the President's House, or the White House, in January 1807. He wrote of his drawing, "Elevation of the South front of the President's house, copied from the design as proposed to be altered in 1807."

As secretary of state, James Madison handled all the correspondence and interviews with foreign diplomats. Part of this duty was to entertain all those diplomats. He gladly handed this chore to Dolley to perform, and she was happy to accept the responsibility.

There was something about Dolley Madison that made her sparkle at social events. Some said it was the way she carried herself. Others said it was because all who came to her house were made to feel at home. She certainly took an enthusiastic interest in people she met, and there were few, if any, public occasions when she ever lost her temper. It was not long before she became a leader in Washington society. Diplomats, civil servants, congressmen, senators, members of the cabinet and their ladies, and the well-to-do of Georgetown and Alexandria, two nearby towns, were all eager to experience Dolley's hospitality.

To host such warm and happy social occasions was not an easy thing to do in the years from 1801 to 1809. Europe was at war, and America was afraid it would get pulled into the conflict. It was hard to maintain friendly social relations with French, British, and

After James was appointed secretary of state under Jefferson, the Madisons moved to fashionable F Street, pictured here in an 1817 engraving by Anne-Marguerite-Henriétte Rouillé de Marigny, Baroness Hyde de Neuville. The building on the right was used as a British headquarters in 1814, during the War of 1812.

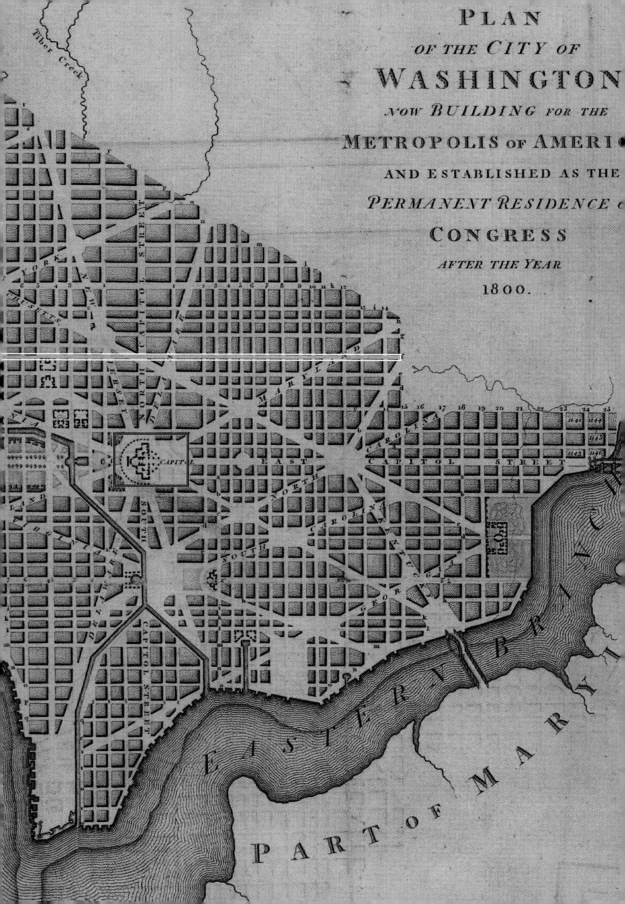

PLAN
OF THE CITY OF
WASHINGTON
NOW BUILDING FOR THE
METROPOLIS OF AMERI
AND ESTABLISHED AS THE
PERMANENT RESIDENCE o
CONGRESS
AFTER THE YEAR
1800.

Spanish diplomats. It was also difficult to maintain a balance between all the feuding politicians in Washington. It took all of Dolley's charm, warmth, and generosity of spirit to keep the peace.

One incident that had a lasting effect on Dolley Madison was President Jefferson's experiment with etiquette, called his rule of pell mell. The first two presidents, George Washington and John Adams, had adopted a version of European court manners. Jefferson, however, considered such formal conduct ill-suited to the United States. He thought Europeans were obsessed with titles and rank. In his view, these foreigners spent endless hours thinking about whose rank was higher. There were, however, no dukes or princes in America, and both rich and poor men used the title "Mr." Only military officers, judges, and ministers were called anything else, and those titles were simply general, colonel, judge, or preacher. Jefferson thought through the problem of how American government officials should conduct themselves in social situations with European diplomats.

Jefferson made a decision. He felt it was so important that he wrote it down. He declared, "In social circles all are equal, whether in, or out, of office, foreign or domestic; & the same equality exists among ladies as among gentlemen."

_____

Previous spread: This map, created by Benjamin Baker and printed by William Bent in 1793, shows a plan of the city of Washington. Georgetown is outlined in blue, the President's House is outlined in pink, the Capitol in red, and F Street in yellow.

It was at a dinner in 1804 that Jefferson's new rule was put to the test. The British had finally sent a minister to the United States, Anthony Merry. He came with his wife, Elizabeth. This was an important statement, because before that the British had sent a low-level official to represent them in the United States.

Jefferson, meanwhile, had decided that he would be entirely informal in his con-duct to the new minister. He greeted Merry in old corduroy trousers and bedroom slip-

Gilbert Stuart painted a portrait of Anthony Merry in 1805, a year after the disastrous dinner hosted by Thomas Jefferson. A copy of the portrait is shown above.

pers, rather than in a fancy suit. This made Merry angry. Jefferson then went further when he invited the Merrys to dinner. According to the rules of diplomatic entertaining, Jefferson should have offered his arm to Elizabeth Merry, as the wife of the guest of honor, and led her into dinner. He did not do so. Instead, he gave his arm to Dolley Madison, who often served as hostess for his dinners. No one stepped in to make amends, and Anthony Merry ended up taking his own wife into the dining room. The Merrys were furious. The Madisons made it even worse when they did the same thing at their home a few days later. The Merrys decided not to accept any more invitations, and Anthony Merry wrote his government to complain of his treatment. It became an international incident.

The Merry affair, as it came to be known, reinforced two things that Dolley had already learned. Social occasions could be dangerous events, and a single misstep could have drastic political consequences. There must be a way to create an American social scene that would combine American simplicity and equality with European elegance and dignity. Dolley Madison would soon have a chance to try out her ideas.

There were moving private moments, as well as important public ones, during Thomas Jefferson's two terms as president of the United States. Dolley's sister Anna, whom Dolley called her "sister-daughter," and who had lived with the Madisons for a decade,

Gilbert Stuart painted this portrait of Richard Cutts around 1804, the year in which Richard married Anna Payne. Richard Cutts lived from 1771 to 1845.

— My dearest Anna the letter from your own
pen was a joyfull one to me as it convinced
me that you must be well — how is our little
tinker, & which is his name ? — I am still in
bed, & can write but badly — you ask me who
is kindest to me here, & I can tell you that
among a numerious sett the Pembertons bear
of the palm — I can never forget Betsy she
has been as you would have been to me —
not a day but I receive additional marks
of hers & Nancy affections — I wish Waddel
would come if he is worthy of Betsy, as she is
too lovely in all respects to be lost by celibicy
— well my dear to our own affairs — my poor
knee is yet but indifferent — so tedious it is to heal
that I am at times lowspirited — yet Doct P says
it will & must soon be well — he has apply'd caustick

[...] seen I wish you which is a
sad thing to feel, but it does every thing that the knife
could do, it removes all impediments to a cure, but it
increases the work of healing & causes this delay —
I have not seen there I am yet, & the longer I stay the
less I care for the vanities of the place — but I shall enjoy
them both two well at last, I suspect — I have not heard
from Polly, but am quite anxious

married Richard Cutts, a Massachusetts congressman from Maine, in 1804. At first, Dolley was so upset that she went into her room and stayed there for days. Her friends came to help her, and soon she was back to being her old social self, although she never stopped missing her sister.

The next year, Dolley was troubled by a painfully ulcerated knee. In August 1805, the Madisons took a coach to Philadelphia to see Dr. Philip Physick, who told Dolley to stay in bed and rest. Luckily, she still had many friends there. She never stopped being social, not even when she was confined to bed. After her knee was successfully treated, she finally returned to Washington in November.

Other events were equally painful. Her youngest brother, John C. Payne, had fallen into bad company and had become an alcoholic and a gambler. To straighten him out, Dolley had him sent to Tripoli in North Africa as secretary to the U.S. consul there. She did not hear from him for years. In 1807, her mother died, and in 1808, her sister Mary passed away. Perhaps few people in Washington knew that Dolley Madison's charming smile concealed so much loss.

Previous page: Dolley Madison wrote this letter to her sister Anna Cutts on August 19, 1805, during the time she spent recovering from her knee operation. She wrote to her sister about her health and how she felt about being back in Philadelphia, the city of her youth, after being away for eight years.

5. Charming and Conciliating

The Republican Party nominated James Madison for president in January 1808. He was Thomas Jefferson's handpicked successor, but that did not make the election easy. In fact, the campaign was besieged with quarrels. Nevertheless, the Madisons hoped to win, and over the spring and summer of 1808, Dolley expansively entertained, as one way to help her husband in his political campaign. On June 3, she wrote her sister Anna Cutts, "We hope from the public prints that we shall not be quite outdone by the Federalists this time."

James won the election and became the fourth president of the United States in 1809. Dolley Madison became the nation's third first lady, and the first truly to preside in the new national capital.

She began with the first inaugural ball ever to be held in Washington, D.C. The city had never seen so large and grand an occasion. People came from places as far away as Baltimore, Maryland, and Richmond, Virginia, and even from New York City, riding in their carriages for days over muddy roads. At seven o'clock that night, the

Possibly the most important contribution that James Madison made as U.S. president was to conduct the nation successfully through the War of 1812. Because this was the first war the nation had fought under the U.S. Constitution, it was proof that a republic could fight a war without stripping its citizens of their civil rights and destroying the balance of power between its three branches of government. Madison did not order foreigners to be expelled from the United States. or critics of the war to be jailed. Newspapers were not shut down, and elections took place as usual during the war. Madison's respect for the law helped the nation weather a war without shredding its constitutional principles.

ball opened. Guests flooded in. An hour later, the band struck up the music to "President Madisons March." The assembly grew quiet, and in walked the Madisons. He was fifty-eight years old, thin and frail, shy in public but witty and talkative in private. He was, moreover, a brilliant man with an enormous capacity for work. She was forty and lovely. Her face was animated and there was a vividness and a beauty about her. The couple stepped into the room. She looked like a queen, in a pale beige velvet dress with a very long train adorned simply with pearls. On her head, she wore a satin turban. The president wore a plain black suit.

There were some who thought all this commotion

Peter Weldon wrote "President Madisons March" around 1809. This song was played at the inaugural ball held by the Madisons after James Madison became the fourth president of the United States in 1809. Several versions of the song were written by different composers for the inaugural ball.

too grand, too much like a European monarchy, for an American republic. The Madisons, however, had made up their minds. They were the heads of the American nation. Their conduct would command the attention of the American people and would define the nation in the eyes of the world.

Dolley was warm and pleasant to everyone, gracious, charming, and welcoming. A good politician, she was cautious and careful. If she had nasty or unpleasant thoughts about other people, she kept them to herself. As her friend Eliza Collins Lee proudly wrote on March 2, there was no question that Dolley Madison was qualified for the job of first lady. For, as Eliza explained, her old friend had "the mind, temper and manners peculiarly fitted for the station, where hospitality and graciousness of deportment, will appear conspicuously charming & conciliating." We should remember those words: "charming and conciliating." They might have served as Dolley Madison's motto.

Almost immediately, she started to work decorating the White House. It was still a brand-new place. Abigail Adams, who had moved there with John Adams in 1800, when it was mostly completed, had found it raw and barren and had hated living there. Thomas Jefferson had finished the structural details of the house, so when the Madisons arrived, the plastering was done, the windows and moldings were in place, and the doors had all been hung. Thomas Jefferson, however, had used his own furniture when he was president. When he left, he took his furniture with him.

The Madisons therefore had to decorate the house not only as their home, but as the official residence of the president. It was the place where diplomats and foreign dignitaries would visit, and they needed to show the world that the new nation was well run. The job of decorating the White House was so important, in fact, that ordinarily the husband, not the wife, would have done it. George Washington chose the paint and the furnishings of his official residence when the government opened in Philadelphia, Pennsylvania. In this case, James Madison knew that his wife had the taste and the talent for the job, and he relied on her to do it well.

Dolley Madison enlisted the help of a well-known architect named Benjamin Henry Latrobe, who was already a good friend. He had married an old companion of hers from Philadelphia, Mary Hazlehurst. Dolley, Benjamin, and Mary worked as a team.

Benjamin Henry Latrobe, here in a portrait by Rembrandt Peale, was a well-known architect.

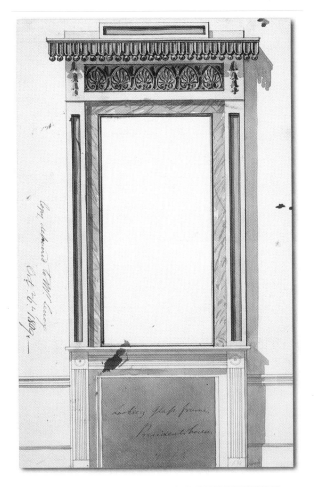

Benjamin Latrobe created this architectural drawing for a looking glass, or mirror, frame to be built for the President's House at the request of Dolley Madison.

They scurried around shops in Washington and Philadelphia, drawing designs, choosing fabrics for drapes, chairs, and sofas, and selecting drawings and paintings to hang on the walls.

They finished the drawing room first because that was the part of the house where the presidential couple would receive their company. The furniture and the draperies were all done in a canary yellow satin, and it was in that bright and cheerful room that Dolley began giving weekly parties. At first people thought that these events were meant only for the richest and most important people in the city. She soon convinced them otherwise. As Benjamin Latrobe wrote to a friend in late June 1809, the third "squeeze," as these parties soon came to be known, was attended "by a perfect rabble in beards and boots."

Dolley was known as the leader of everything fashionable during the time of both Thomas Jefferson's and James Madison's presidencies. Above is Dolley's Empire-style silk-and-velvet ball gown and turban from around 1810. Dolley was not only known for her fashion but also for her support of charities, such as the Washington City Orphan's Asylum, organized by her friend Marcia Burnes van Ness.

It sounds like it would be nice to give lots of parties, and Dolley Madison hosted dinners, card games, and other social events besides her Wednesday night squeezes. Washington politicians, however, were always fighting with one another. Managing all the personalities night after night was quite a challenge. Guests wrote awful things about one another and spread nasty gossip. The diplomats sometimes argued with one another, too, or simply refused to be in the same room at the same time. The city elites, who were neither politicians nor diplomats, but bankers, real estate developers, and newspaper editors, got swept up in all these disputes. Giving parties was not always fun.

The Madisons served their guests using fine china.
This dessert cooler and soup tureen, from around 1806,
were used during James Madison's administration.

Everyone understood, however, that the city needed places to gather, and there were few spots either as large or as grand as the White House. They knew that there had to be a time when ordinary people could see the president. If they came to him during the day, when would he be able to get his work done? Everyone also knew that the issues over which all this quarreling took place really were important. The arguments gave people with differing viewpoints a chance to express their own opinions and to think about the opinions that others expressed.

Most of the critical issues were about foreign relations. There was a war going on in Europe. France and Great Britain were fighting over who would be the most important nation in Europe, with control over world trade. Americans wanted to be neutral and trade with both countries. Both Great Britain and France wanted to stop each other from trading with the United States. They stopped American ships, captured American sailors, and took American goods. James Madison worried about these issues because he felt America had to be independent, but he did not want to lead the country into war.

The international situation put a lot of pressure on American politics. James Madison was never as popular as George Washington or Thomas Jefferson. Even members of James Madison's own administration were split over these issues, while the opposing party, the

Federalists, never tired of criticizing him. The French and British ministers would not talk to each other. Everyone got dragged into this great big mess.

It was Dolley Madison's job to give parties that would bring everyone together to at least talk about the issues. She was very skilled at this task. She walked around her parties with a kind word for everyone, trying to make people feel better about each other. She always carried a book, although she never had time to read from it, so that she would have something to say that did not involve politics.

F. A. A. Dahme created this portrait of James Milnor around 1910. Milnor lived from 1773 to 1844. He was a lawyer, a U.S. representative from Pennsylvania, and a clergyman.

When new members of Congress who were unfriendly to the Madison administration came to her parties for the first time, she found ways to speak to them and to create bonds of friendship. One example was a Federalist congressman from Philadelphia named James Milnor. He had been born a Quaker but had become Episcopalian. After he arrived in Washington, he decided he had to go to one of Dolley Madison's squeezes. He did not want to go, and he expected to dislike Dolley

Madison and her friends, but he felt it was politically important for him to attend. Milnor went, and Dolley gracefully managed to speak to him not just once, but several times during the evening. Later he wrote to his wife that "she had heard of my Quaker extraction, and observed that neither of us were very faithful representatives of that respectable society." They became friends.

She walked a fine line between what the Federalists wanted, what the Republicans needed, and what the foreign diplomats expected. She did not always succeed, but she tried hard and usually did an excellent job of putting everyone at ease. As one of her contemporaries wrote, Dolley Madison had "dignity, sweetness, and grace. It seems to me that such manners would disarm envy itself, & conciliate even enemies." In this seemingly simple skill lay much of her greatness.

6. "The Tunesian Sabre within my reach"

It was an early summer day, June 15, 1811, when Dolley Madison took a moment from her busy schedule to write to her cousin Edward Coles. The two were close, and Edward was James Madison's secretary. He made copies and filed the papers of the president. It was an important job, but during the break between congressional sessions, Edward had gone on a trip north. So Dolley penned him a note. It was chatty and full of local news, but toward the bottom of it, she issued him a brief warning. "I have no doubt, but that Congress will be called before November."

Almost as if she were whispering a secret, Dolley sent her cousin

Edward Coles served as James Madison's secretary from 1809 to 1815. He went on to become Illinois's governor (1822–1826). This portrait was based on an 1852 painting by J. H. Brown.

Opposite: William Chappell created this engraving of Dolley Payne Madison around 1812.

an indirect, but firm, instruction: Come home soon! She was telling him, without really saying it, that the president did not think that the United States would be able to stay out of the war much longer. He would have to call Congress into session early to prepare the nation, and Edward, Dolley was saying, needed to be there to oversee the paperwork and assist her husband.

She was, of course, correct. She talked to her husband, and she did what she could to help him. She knew that bringing his personal assistant back to Washington was one way she could aid her husband. On July 24, 1811, James Madison issued a proclamation calling Congress to meet one month early, on November 4. A little more than six months after that, on June 18, 1812, the U.S. Congress declared war against Great Britain. The War of 1812 had begun.

Great Britain was a powerful nation with a large army and a splendid navy. The United States, on the other hand, was a minor country with enormous boundaries to defend. It bordered the British colony of Canada to the north, the Spanish colonies of Florida and Texas to the south and west, and the Atlantic Ocean to the east. The United States was helped by the fact that Great Britain was already at war with France and most British forces were tied up in the struggle against Napoleon. What hurt the United States was a combination of three things. First, there were political divisions within the nation. Most New Englanders did not want to fight

England at all. Second, the United States had a weak army and navy. Third, the distances within the United States were vast and the roads were poor, so it was difficult to keep the army supplied efficiently with food, clothing, and arms.

Dolley Madison followed the progress of the war with keen interest from the very beginning. The president thought an invasion of Canada was the logical place to begin the war. Canada was a British colony. James Madison told the governor of the Michigan territory, General William Hull, to attack. The attack was a disaster. By early August, Hull withdrew his forces in defeat. When Dolley Madison heard the news, she was furious. The Madisons were on their way to Montpelier when, as Dolley wrote Edward Coles on August 31, 1812, "an Express overtook us, with the melancholy tidings,

General William Hull, here in a portrait by James Sharples Sr. created between 1795 and 1800, had fought in the American Revolution. He led a failed attack on Canada during the War of 1812.

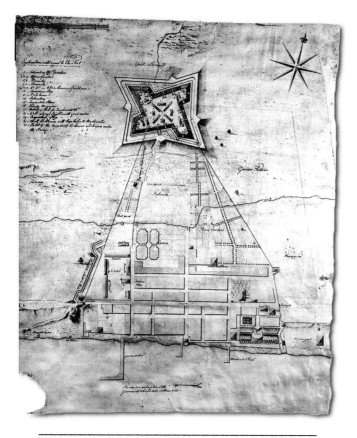

Fort Detroit is pictured here in a 1799 sketch. The British began their attack on Fort Detroit, on August 15, 1812. At first Hull refused to give up. During the night, however, the British and their Native American allies surrounded the fort. Hull, fearing a massacre, surrendered.

that Genl. Hull had surrender'd Detroit, himself & the whole Army to the British! Do you not tremble with resentment, at this treacherous act?"

In the beginning, the war did not go well for the United States. Although they won some important victories, the future of the nation continued to be in peril. Dolley Madison was an ardent patriot, and she believed that the United States could win the war. The fighting on the Canadian frontier, however, was remote. Fort Detroit, where General William Hull had surrendered, was 500 miles (805 km) away. However, when the British navy attacked Americans around Chesapeake Bay in 1813, the war moved close to home. Dolley Madison became even more defiant. "I have always been an advocate for fighting when assailed," she wrote to her cousin Edward Coles. "I therefore keep the old Tunesian Sabre within my reach."

The British left Chesapeake Bay in 1813, but a year later, on August 19, 1814, they landed another force there and started to march toward Washington, D.C. Local citizens fled in fear and condemned the administration for not protecting them. Dolley Madison was disgusted at their cowardice. She would not be driven from her home.

On June 6, 1814, a strong American fleet commanded by Commodore Joshua Barney, a native of Baltimore, was attacked by the boats of the British squadron in the Chesapeake Bay under the command of Captain Robert Barrie. He was hoping to draw them out of their harbor to be attacked by his supporting ships. He did not succeed in his plan.

The British troops began walking toward Washington. At first they marched slowly. It was August, and hot. The British soldiers wore heavy uniforms and carried burdensome packs and weapons. It was hard to believe they were serious about attacking Washington. President Madison kept thinking the British would not strike at the capital. On they came, however, and on August 22, he finally left the city and rode out to Bladensburg, Maryland, to review the American troops. The first lady stayed on in the White House. On August 23, she wrote to her sister Anna that she had received two letters from her husband since his departure. She wrote, "the last is the most alarming, because he desires I should be ready at a moment's warning to enter my carriage and leave the city; that the enemy seemed stronger than had been reported, and that it might happen that they would reach the city, with the intention to destroy it."

With the enemy drawing near, Dolley prepared to leave. "Since sunrise," she wrote to her sister, "I have been turning my spy-glass in every direction and watching with unwearied anxiety." In expectation of the attack, she filled a wagon with valuable documents and sent it off for safekeeping at the Bank of Maryland. Then, against the advice of messengers and friends who stopped by to warn her to depart, she decided she must complete one more task: to save the portrait of George Washington hanging in the White House. It was screwed into the wall, and no one could take it down.

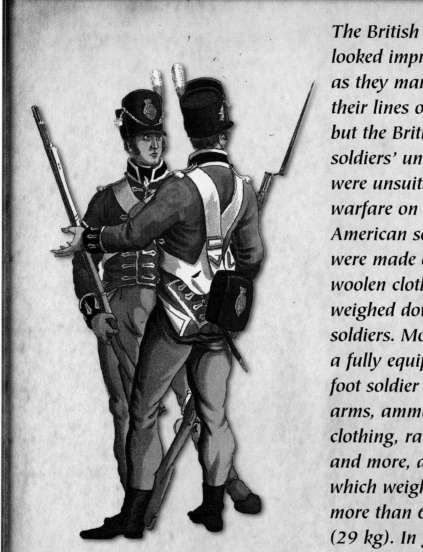

"Privates of the First Regiment of Foot Guards on Service" from *Costume of the Army of the British Empire, according to the last regulations, 1814,* was published in 1815 by Charles Hamilton Smith.

The British soldiers looked impressive as they marched in their lines of red, but the British soldiers' uniforms were unsuitable for warfare on American soil. They were made of coarse woolen cloth that weighed down the soldiers. Moreover, a fully equipped foot soldier carried arms, ammunition, clothing, rations, and more, all of which weighed more than 65 lbs (29 kg). In general, the British soldiers were hot and uncomfortable as they fought.

She decided on a shortcut. "I have ordered the frame to be broken, and the canvass taken out." It was done. She gave the precious portrait to friends for safekeeping. Then she fled, writing to her sister "And now, dear sister, I must leave this house. . . . When I shall write you again, or where I shall be tomorrow I cannot tell!!" Within hours the British arrived and burned down the White House, leaving just the shell. The Madisons' personal belongings were destroyed, including their clothes and their furniture.

The British moved on to Baltimore. Warned ahead of time, the city was prepared and the British failed to take it. Francis Scott Key celebrated the American victory in his poem, "Defense of Fort McHenry," which would later be adapted as "The Star-Spangled Banner."

Dolley Madison was the heroine of the War of 1812. first lady Dolley Madison had been brave enough to confront the British. She had also had the presence of mind to save what she could from the White House. A true patriot, she had protected what belonged to the nation.

The Madisons never returned to the White House to live. The fire had gutted the building, and it took years to rebuild it. Little remained of the beautiful decorations with which she and the Latrobes had filled the

Opposite: Dolley Madison saved this portrait of George Washington from being destroyed by the British during the War of 1812. Gilbert Stuart painted this oil portrait of Washington in 1800. This painting is important because it was one of the first that showed Washington as the president of a new nation rather than as a military hero.

William Strickland created this color aquatint after
George Munger, called *A View of the Capitol of the
United States after the Conflagration of the 24th August 1814.*

presidential mansion. The following December, Dolley
wrote to her old friend Mrs. Latrobe of her sadness at
all that beauty lost. "Two hours before the enemy
entered the city," she reminisced, "I left the house
where Mr. Latrobe's elegant taste had been justly
admired, and where you and I had so often wandered
together." She went on, writing that it would tire Mrs.
Latrobe "to read the list of my losses." The president
and the first lady moved to the Octagon House on New

Previous spread: This image of the capture of Washington, D.C., in
1814 was published in Rapin de Thoyras's 1815 *History of England*.

Coltman's Bill	$34.73.
Kleibus "	135.48.
Fallon's Bill	34.62.
Kennedy's Bill	6.50.
McGrath's "	21.—
Forton's "	3.—
Johnson's "	5.25.
Cheats Bill	83.62.
Miller's Bill	80.68.
Shaw & Birth	28.29.
Yeatis Bill	46.25.
Miller's Bill	46.23.—
Coyle's Bill	37.05.
Randolph's Bill	57.08.
Hollenbach's Bill	7.20.
Hornsby's "	18.—
Lakette's Bill	116.42.
	$753.40.

In the wake of the burning of the White House in August 1814, Dolley Madison concerned herself with the cost of repairs to the White House and the purchase of new furniture. George Boyd sent her a letter on September 2, 1816, that detailed some of the expenses involved.

The Madisons briefly lived at the Octagon House, pictured above, on New York Avenue before moving to the house on 19th Street and Pennsylvania Avenue.

York Avenue briefly and then to a house on the corner of 19th Street and Pennsylvania Avenue. She refurbished it with secondhand goods, and she went on entertaining.

James and Dolley Madison's years in Washington ended in triumph and glory. In 1815, the Americans signed a peace treaty with Great Britain. Political conflict came to an end. There was a general feeling of goodwill and success. The United States had secured the rights of Americans in what has often been called the Second War of Independence. James Madison retired from the presidency in 1817, and he and Dolley returned to Montpelier.

7. "Nursing and Comforting my patient"

On an April day in 1817, Dolley Madison gazed over the steamboat railing as the banks of the Potomac River slid by. The inauguration of President James Monroe, the Georgetown ball in Dolley's honor, and endless hours of packing were over. The Madisons were finally on their way home to Montpelier. James Madison, "freed from the cares of public life," was excited and wandered about the boat, "talking and jesting with everyone on board." Dolley's reaction was more complicated.

Washington had been Dolley Madison's home for the past sixteen years. Her family and friends lived there, or at least gathered

President James Monroe, pictured in this 1816 portrait by John Vanderlyn, became president after James Madison.

there when Congress was in session. Moreover, she had been the leader of Washington society. It had been hard but rewarding work, and she had been good at it. Now she would no longer be mistress of Washington society, but simply mistress of Montpelier.

The plantation home she would take charge of was somewhat larger than when she had lived there in the 1790s. During James's presidency, the Madisons had expanded the house yet again to accommodate more guests and to give it a grander appearance. James's mother, Nelly Conway Madison, still lived in one side of the house with her slaves and her own schedule. The relationship between Dolley and her mother-in-law was a caring and an affectionate one. At one point, Nelly Madison turned to Dolley and said, "You are my Mother now, and take care of me in my old age."

The Madisons practiced Virginia hospitality, which meant that not only family and friends but also strangers were invited to eat and sleep under their roof. It was not unusual for twenty people to sit down to dinner, especially in the summers when Dolley's sister Anna Cutts and her family came for their annual two-month stay.

The dinners were splendid, too. One visitor wrote that "good soups, flesh, fish and vegetables, well cooked—desert and excellent wines of various kinds" crowded the table and satisfied the guests' appetites. The Madisons lived well.

Nelly Rose Conway Madison, pictured here in a 1799 portrait by Charles Peale Polk, was James Madison's mother. She gave birth to eleven children, seven of whom lived to adulthood. When Nelly was in poor health, Dolley Madison cared for her. Nelly Conway Madison was 98 when she died.

Gilbert Stuart painted Anna Payne Cutts around 1804, the year in which she married Richard Cutts. Anna lived from 1779 to 1832.

Dolley spent a good part of her day supervising work in the house and the kitchen and working in her garden. Along with vegetables for the table, the plantation produced grapes, figs, apples, cherries, and peaches. From the peaches James distilled brandy, which he proudly offered to his guests. Dolley also cured bacon and put up salt pork. She wrote during one of James's absences that "I am too busy a House keeper to become a poetess in my solitude." It was a busy and happy retirement.

There were a few clouds, however, gathering over that sunny landscape. Tobacco and wheat harvests in the 1820s had been bad in Virginia, and the prices for these crops had fallen all over the country. That meant the Madisons had to dip into their savings to pay for their needs. Prices for land fell as well, and when James tried to sell some of his property, he found few buyers.

James Madison is shown here in an 1875 portrait by Catherine Drinker
modeled on Gilbert Stuart's painting. After he retired, the Madisons
continued to entertain. However, they had to support many family
members, and it became hard to pay their own debts and expenses.

People had no money to pay their debts, so money owed to the Madisons was not repaid. James eventually had to take out a bank loan.

There were other financial demands on the Madisons. Dolley's son, John Payne Todd, had never settled down. Between short stays at Montpelier, Dolley's son would disappear for long periods, shuttling between Washington, Philadelphia, and New York, drinking, gambling, and piling up large debts. He expected his mother and stepfather to pay them, because they always had. Over the years, James Madison spent about $40,000, an immense amount in those days, to cover Todd's debts.

John Payne Todd was Dolley Madison's only surviving son. This 1830 or 1840 image is based on a lost miniature on ivory, possibly by Henry Kurtz, engraver and landscape painter. It is the only surviving likeness of John Payne Todd.

James had paid some of that money in secret, but his wife knew enough "to make her wretched the whole time of his [John Payne Todd's] strange absence and mysterious silence." Finally, in the summer of 1829,

Dolley Madison's son, John Payne, was probably held in this Philadelphia prison, or in one like it. This is the jail on Walnut Street in which debtors and criminals were held. This image, engraved by W. Birch and his son Thomas, was published by R. Cambell & Company.

Dolley found out that her son was being held in a Philadelphia debtor's prison. "My pride, my sensibility, and every feeling of my soul is wounded," she wrote to her sister Anna.

Anna's husband, Richard Cutts, was also in trouble. He had lost his fortune during the War of 1812, and had supported his family since then with loans and a government job. In the early 1820s, Cutts declared bankruptcy. The money that the Madisons had loaned him was lost. James bought the Cutts' home on Lafayette

This is the home that James Madison purchased for Richard
and Anna Cutts. It is located at 1518 H Street Northwest,
in Washington, D.C. They had lived there for many years but
could no longer afford to pay for it after declaring bankruptcy.
Madison bought it so that they could remain in their home.

Square in Washington, D.C., and arranged for the family to continue to live there.

Despite their troubles, the Madisons took comfort in each other. During the long winter months at Montpelier, when the cold rains fell, James and Dolley would sit before the fire, read, and play chess. Dolley loved novels and poetry. James read history and politics. They also worked to arrange and copy his letters, essays, and speeches. He wanted Dolley to have them published after his death, especially the notes he had taken during the Constitutional Convention in 1787. There had been a lot of interest in them over the years, and he thought they would provide Dolley with an income after he was gone.

In 1830, James had his first bad attack of rheumatism. His fingers and legs grew twisted and painful. By March 1832, he was weak and bedridden. Dolley was his constant nurse. "I never leave him, more than a few minutes at a time," she wrote to a friend, "and have not left the enclosure around our house for the last eight months." In August 1832, another blow struck. Dolley's beloved sister Anna died.

Despite Madison's illness, a parade of famous people came to visit at Montpelier. James would lie on his daybed and converse with Henry Clay, President Andrew Jackson, Harriet Martineau, and Frances Wright. All wanted to share ideas with "the great little Madison" and to partake of Dolley's famed hospitality.

Harriet Martineau, shown here in an engraving published in the October 1876 issue of *Harper's* new monthly magazine, wrote many articles, books, and pamphlets about political and social issues, including the rights of women.

A series of fevers and rheumatic attacks over the next two years weakened James Madison to the point of death. Dolley confided to one of her friends, "My days are devoted to nursing and comforting my patient." Dolley Madison continued to write her husband's letters through his final days. On June 28, 1836, James Madison died.

8. "A very hearty, good looking woman"

Dolley Madison barely had time to grieve for her husband. She was the executrix of his estate and so was responsible for paying his debts and his bequests. James Madison had planned to publish his papers. He intended those proceeds to pay sums to his nieces and nephews, Princeton University, the University of Virginia, and other organizations. The total amounted to about $15,000.

While her brother John supervised the copying of Madison's manuscripts, Dolley asked her friends for advice about contacting publishers. The news they wrote to her was not good. Few book publishers were interested in her project, and those who were did not offer enough money.

Dolley was crushed. She knew that her friends and the nation expected the Madison Papers to appear. She felt that she had disappointed her husband. In September 1836, she suffered "a painful inflammation of the eyes, which brought on chills and fevers, and her general health became so bad . . . that she could not walk alone."

James Madison willed his library to the University of Virginia, pictured here in an engraving by William Goodacre. The University of Virginia was founded by Thomas Jefferson in 1819.

For years she had taken care of her husband, her son, and her brother and sisters. Now, when she needed someone to care for her, there was no one to take charge of her affairs. Her niece and companion, Anna Payne, looked after her and nursed her. The big decisions, however, had to be made by Dolley alone.

In January 1837, Dolley eagerly agreed to a suggestion by one of her friends that she sell the three volumes of Madison's manuscripts to Congress. The sale was made for $30,000, enough for Dolley to pay James's bequests.

James Madison wrote this letter, partially in code, to Thomas Jefferson on May 23, 1789. Madison reported on the opening of the new federal government and was particularly critical of efforts in the Senate to set an aristocratic tone in the legislature. Madison feared this approach would damage the new republican type of government.

Immediately her health began to improve, and she began to look forward to visiting Washington, D.C., later that year.

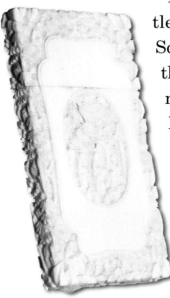

By November 1837, she was resettled in her house on Lafayette Square, reacquainting herself with the Washington social scene. She made sixty-five social visits in December alone and attended a number of balls, parties, and teas that winter. She dined at all the finest houses, including twice at the White House with President Martin Van Buren.

Many people wrote to her. Some people requested her autograph; others asked to be allowed to dedicate plays and poems to her. Many wrote letters requesting her help in finding jobs for themselves, relations, or friends. "I have now more letters piled upon my table than I can answer," she wrote one February day, "and more engagements at home and abroad than I can perform."

Dolley's ivory calling card case was found in 1956 by a man named Charles Hafner, who was hired to clean out a house in the estate of Neva Kunkel, a distant relative of Dolley's.

She enjoyed her role as one of Washington's most sought-after guests. One gentleman described meeting her at a dinner: "The old lady is a very hearty, good looking woman of about 75 . . . I paid her the same attentions I should have done a girl of 15— which seemed to suit her fancy very well." Each year on New Year's Day, there were two receptions that everybody wanted to attend: the open houses at the White House and at Dolley Madison's house.

By 1840, however, Dolley was feeling a financial pinch. She had made some unwise investments over the years, and

Mathew Brady took this photograph of Dolley Madison and her niece, Annie Payne, on July 4, 1848. This photograph was found in a trunk in the home of a descendant of Dolley's niece and now is held by the Greensboro Historical Museum in North Carolina.

she had taken out loans she could not pay back. Montpelier still was not making a profit. The country was in a depression, and credit was tight. People to whom she owed money began to take her to court. To make matters worse, her son John Payne Todd continued his spendthrift ways.

In the spring of 1823, Dolley Madison wrote a letter to her son that included local gossip and some advice on how John Payne might receive cash to pay his gambling debts. She was disappointed with his bad habits, but she loved him and wanted him to do well.

For the next few years, Dolley stayed at Montpelier, hoping to save enough money to pay off her debts. In order to raise cash, she rented out her Washington home. She even tried to arrange the publication of the last collection of James Madison's manuscripts. This was unsuccessful.

With no other alternative, she sold Montpelier in August 1844. She wrote to the buyer, Henry W. Moncure, "No one I think, can appreciate my feeling of grief and dismay at the necessity of transferring to another a beloved home." It was a sad day. The Madison family had lived at Montpelier for more than 100 years.

It was a sadder day for the Madison slaves. Some had been deeded to John Payne Todd. Others would continue to live with Dolley. The bulk of the slaves who had called Montpelier home would be kept or sold as the new master decided. There had been no plan to free them at James Madison's death. Now Dolley could not have freed them if she wanted to.

From 1844 until her death, Dolley made her home in Washington. Her money problems continued until Congress finally bought the last collection of the Madison Papers in 1848. Three old friends of Dolley's held the money in trust for her, giving her the interest to live on.

Next spread: Montgomery C. Meigs created this sketch on September 22, 1850, of the Washington Monument under construction. Construction began in 1848, but the monument was not opened to the public until 1888. *Inset*: This is what the 555-foot (169-m) building looks like today.

Wash. Monument 24 Sept '6?

Dolley Madison was confirmed as an Episcopalian at St. John's Church, above, in 1845. This historic building is located at the corner of 16th and H Streets in Washington, D.C.

She continued to be seen at many social occasions. Dolley was constant in her attendance at St. John's Episcopal Church. She was confirmed there in 1845. As the widow of one of those men who led the country to independence and helped to create a new nation, she was invited in July 1848 to participate in the laying of the cornerstone of the Washington Monument. She declined because of the immense crowds, but watched the festivities from the White House.

In the spring of 1849, she fell into periods of sickness that weakened her. By July, she had taken to her bed. On July 12, she died, in the words of her nephew, "without a struggle or apparent pain, . . . at peace with her maker, and with all the world and it with her."

9. "All the ladies of Virginia"

Dolley Madison's funeral was held on Saturday, July 14, 1849, at St. John's Episcopal Church. At four o'clock that afternoon, the rector gave the eulogy. An hour later, Zachary Taylor, president of the United States, conducted the procession that took her body to Congressional Cemetery in Washington, D.C., where it would remain until it could be removed to Montpelier. There she would finally rest beside James Madison, her beloved husband of forty-two years.

Five days after the funeral, an unidentified woman sent a note to the local Washington newspaper calling for "all the ladies of Virginia, wherever they may be" to wear a black armband for thirty days. The letter said that the women of Virginia should show the world how much they mourned this great Virginian. Her admirer explained

---

Next page: Dolley Madison's death affected many people. Through her charm and grace, she had become a friend and favorite among all who knew her. Many articles were printed about her death and funeral, such as these from the *Daily National Intelligencer*.

Daily National Intelligencer.

WASHINGTON.

"Liberty and Union, now and forever, one and inseparable."

SATURDAY, JULY 14, 1849.

It is with saddened hearts that we announce to our readers the decease of Mrs. MADISON, Widow of JAMES MADISON, Ex-President of the United States. She died at her residence in this city on Thursday night last, the 12th instant, between 10 and 11 o'clock, aged about eighty-two years.

Beloved by all who personally knew her, and universally respected, this venerable Lady closed her long and well-spent life with the calm resignation which goodness of heart combined with piety only can impart. It would seem an abuse of terms to say that we regret the departure of one so ripe and so fitted for a better world. But in the case of this excellent Lady, she continued until within a few weeks to grace society with her presence, and lend to it those graces with which she adorned the circles of the greatest, the wisest, and best, during the bright career of her illustrious husband. Wherever she appeared, every one became conscious of the presence of a spirit of benignity and gentleness, united to all the attributes of feminine loveliness. For ourselves, whose privilege it was to know and admire her through the last forty years of her life, it would not be easy to speak in terms of exaggeration of the graces and winning manners of this eminent Lady. To attempt it would add no brightness to her fair fame, and would be little needed to move the public sympathy. All of our own country and thousands in other lands will need no language of eulogy to inspire a deep and sincere regret when they learn the demise of one who touched all hearts by her goodness and won the admiration of all by the charms of dignity and grace.

FROM THE RICHMOND WHIG OF YESTERDAY.

MRS. MADISON.

"Honor to whom honor is due."

It is proposed to the Ladies of Richmond, and to the ladies of *Virginia, wheresoever* they may be, that for days they shall wear upon the left arm a bow of black as a tribute of respect to the memory of their esteemed patriot, Mrs. MADISON; of *her* who has done credit sex, by her _____ _____ _____ the duties and of her stati _____ the terms _____

She dese_____ who are w_____ the sable _____

FUNERAL OF THE LATE MRS. MADISON.

The remains of the venerable relict of Ex-President MADISON were removed from her late residence, in Lafayette square, to St. John's Church yesterday afternoon at 4 o'clock. The Rev. Mr. PYNE, Rector of the Church, delivered, in a very feeling manner, an eloquent and just eulogy on the character of the deceased _____

with dee_____
ding the _____
binet Off_____
the May_____
guished _____
FRENCH _____
ral solemn_____
neral proc_____
moved from_____
where the _____
to its final _____

WASHINGTON.

"Liberty and Union, now and forever, one and inseparable."

MONDAY, JULY 16, 1849.

FUNERAL OF MRS. MADISON.

The Funeral of Mrs. MADISON will take place this afternoon, at 4 o'clock, from St. John's Church. The following is the order of the procession adopted by the friends of the family:

The Reverend Clergy.
Attending Physicians.

PALL BEARERS.

Hon. J. M. Clayton,	Hon. W. M. Meredith,
Mr. Gales,	Mr. Ritchie,
General Jesup,	General Totten,
Com. Morris,	Com. Warrington,
General Henderson,	Mr. Pleasonton,
Gen. Walter Jones,	Mr. Fendall.

The Family.
The President and Cabinet.
The Diplomatic Corps.
Members of the Senate and House of Representatives at present in Washington, and their officers.
Judges of the Supreme Court and Courts of the District, and their officers.
Officers of the Army and Navy.
Mayor and Corporation of Washington.
Citizens and Strangers.

that Dolley Madison was a true American. She had done credit to her sex by performing all of the duties of a first lady with grace and dignity. Dolley Madison should be honored.

Dolley died a decade before the Civil War began. When the war ended, the American people were looking for emblems of unity and peace and new ways to understand the principles upon which the United States of America had been founded. Writers tended to

Dolley's grave at Montpelier is pictured above. She is buried beside her husband.

focus mostly on men, but a few, especially women authors, wrote about Dolley Madison. She had never been forgotten, but now she became important as a southern woman who had played a unifying role during her husband's presidency and had been a national heroine in the War of 1812. In the 1880s, her grand-niece published a book of her letters.

By the early twentieth century, there were more and more biographies published about her. She was a great national figure. She had led the kind of life that seemed admirable to many women and men. She had been gracious and well mannered, dignified and charitable. She was famous for decorating the greatest home in America, the White House. She was known as a wonderful hostess. She had always served the interests of her husband. She was a strong woman who exercised her influence in ways that were appropriate for her era.

There were books, stories, novels, and plays written about her. In the late nineteenth century, companies started using her name and employing pictures of her to advertise new products. By the 1920s, there were a lot of things named for Dolley Madison. Cakes and ice cream are the most famous, but there were Dolley Madison shoes and hats, stockings and makeup, luggage and bedspreads, silverware and glassware, streets and boulevards, and hotels and motels. Her name was usually misspelled "Dolly" on these products. Dolley Madison

Opposite: William S. Elwell painted this portrait of Dolley Madison in 1848, the year before she died. He later sold the portrait to Dolley's friend William Winston Seaton, editor and co-owner of the Washington, D.C., *National Intelligencer.* Dolley Madison was described by Elwell in his diary as "a very Estimable lady kind & obliging, one of the Old School."

Above is just one example of a product that carried Dolley Madison's name. This quart-size milk bottle from Richmond Dairy dates from the late 1930s and has a Dolly Madison ice cream advertisement on the back.

remained important and well known both because she was a heroine and a great first lady, and because there were so many household items that carried her name.

After the 1960s, most of the products that had been labeled for her were no longer used, or the companies went out of business, or they changed their product names. She remains, however, an important American woman, and it becomes increasingly clear that she played a larger role in America's history than simply serving as the wife of the fourth U.S. president. Today we care more about the role of the American first lady. As we increasingly study the history of the first lady, we always come back to Dolley Madison. She set the model for what a first lady should be. We remain indebted to her legacy.

Timeline

1768 On May 20, Dolley Payne is born in North Carolina.

1769 The Paynes move to Virginia.

1790 On January 7, Dolley Payne marries John Todd Jr., a young Philadelphian lawyer.

1792 On February 29, Dolley gives birth to her first child, John Payne Todd.

1793 Dolley Payne Todd's second child, William Temple Todd, is born.

 An outbreak of yellow fever in Philadelphia kills her husband's parents, her husband, and her second child in October.

1794 In May, Dolley Payne Todd, now a young widow, meets James Madison, a congressman from Virginia.

 On September 15, Dolley and James wed at the home of Lucy Payne Washington.

1797 James Madison retires from the U.S. House

of Representatives and brings his family back to Montpelier, the Madison plantation in Orange County, Virginia.

1800   Thomas Jefferson is elected president of the United States.

1801   Jefferson appoints James Madison his secretary of state, and in June, the family moves to Washington, D.C.

1803   Dolley Madison plays hostess for presidential dinners.

1804   Dolley hosts the first Merry affair.

1805   Dolley Madison suffers from an ulcerated knee.

1809   James Madison is inaugurated as fourth president of the United States.

1812   On June 1, Madison sends a war message to Congress. War is declared on June 18.

1813   James Madison is inaugurated for his second term as president of the United States. Later that year, he becomes seriously ill.

The Madisons send Payne Todd to Europe as secretary to the American peace mission to Britain.

1814   On August 24, the British burn the White

House. Dolley Madison saves the silver, the official papers, the red curtains, and Gilbert Stuart's portrait of George Washington.

1815   War with Great Britain is ended by the Treaty of Ghent. Payne Todd returns from Europe, having run up a debt in excess of $6,500.

1817   James Madison leaves office, and the Madisons return to Montpelier.

1829   James and Dolley Madison go to Richmond for three months, where James sits as member of the convention to revise the Virginia state constitution.

John Payne Todd is threatened with prison for his ever-growing debts. James Madison pays his stepson's debts.

1836   James Madison dies.

1837   Dolley Madison tries to publish her husband's papers. The U.S. Congress pays $30,000 to purchase his notes on the Constitutional Convention.

Dolley Madison moves back to Washington, D.C., with her niece Anna Payne.

1839   Dolley Madison moves back to Montpelier

to run the plantation, but fails to make a profit.

1841   Dolley Madison again returns to Washington, D.C.

1842   Dolley Madison tries to publish more of James's papers. She mortgages her house and sells part of the Montpelier plantation.

1844   The U.S. House of Representatives honors Dolley Madison with a permanent seat the halls of Congress.

From the White House, she dictates the first personal message sent by telegraphy.

She sells the rest of Montpelier.

1848   Congress finally purchases the rest of James Madison's papers for $25,000. Of this sum, $20,000 is invested in a trust fund for Dolley.

Dolley Madison serves as honorary chair of a women's group to raise funds for the Washington Memorial.

1849   On July 12, Dolley Madison dies. The funeral is held on July 14.

Glossary

bequest (bih-KWEST) A gift that is willed to you.

Bill of Rights (BIL UV RYTS) The first ten amendments to the U.S. Constitution.

burdensome (BUR-duhn-sum) Something that makes you worry, like a duty or responsibility.

commotion (kuh-MOH-shun) Noisy confusion.

Constitutional Convention (kon-stih-TOO-shuh-nul kuhn-VEN-shun) The political body that met in the summer of 1787 to create the U.S. Constitution.

Continental Congress (kon-tihn-EN-tuhl KON-gres) The political body that directed the American Revolution.

cultivate (KUHL-tih-vayt) To grow, as in, to cultivate tobacco.

delegate (DEH-lih-get) A member of a political body, as in a delegate to the Continental Congress.

diplomat (DIH-pluh-mat) A person who represents his or her country's interests in a foreign country.

etiquette (EH-tih-kit) The manners to be observed in social life.

eulogy (YOO-luh-jee) A speech of praise, usually given at a funeral.

executrix (ek-ZEH-kyuh-triks) A woman who settles the legal affairs of a dead person.

extraction (ek-STRAK-shun) A person's family and national background.

Federalists (FEH-duh-ruh-lists) Originally those who supported the U.S. Constitution. It soon came to mean those people who supported a strong active government and a large army and navy.

legacy (LEH-guh-see) Something received from the past.

manumit (man-yuh-MIT) Set free.

minister (MIH-nuh-ster) A diplomat one grade below ambassador.

refurbish (ree-FUR-bish) To make over, or renovate.

republicans (rih-PUH-blih-kens) People who supported a less powerful government, fewer taxes, and little or no army or navy.

sabre (SAY-bur) A cavalry sword. Dolley Madison had been given one by the ruler of Tunis.

spendthrift (SPEND-thrift) Wasteful with money.

suitor (SOO-tur) One who seeks to marry a woman.

turban (TUR-buhn) A headdress made of a cap, around which is wound a long cloth.

ulcerated (UHL-sur-ayt-ed) To have an ulcer, or open sore.

wheelwrights (WEEL-ryts) People who make and repair wheels.

Additional Resources

Books

Pflueger, Lynda. *Dolley Madison: Courageous First Lady,* Historical American Biographies. Berkeley Heights, New Jersey: Enslow Publishers, 1999.

Davidson, Mary. *Dolley Madison: Famous First Lady* A Discovery Biography. Philadelphia: Chelsea House Publishers, 1992.

Web Sites

Due to the changing nature of Internet links, PowerPlus Books has developed an online list of Web sites related to the subject of this book. This site is updated regularly. Please use this link to access the list:

www.powerkidslinks.com/lalt/madison/

Bibliography

Anthony, Katherine Susan. *Dolley Madison, Her Life and Times*. New York: Doubleday & Company, Inc., 1949.

Ketcham, Ralph. *James Madison: A Biography*. Charlottesville, Virginia: Macmillan, 1990.

Mattern, David and Holly Shulman, eds. *The Selected Letters of Dolley Madison*. Charlottesville, Virginia: University of Virginia Press, 2003.

Shulman, Holly. "Dolley Payne Todd Madison." In *American First Ladies: Their Lives and Their Legacy*, edited by Lewis L. Gould. New York: Routledge, 2001.

Index

About the Authors

David B. Mattern is Research Associate Professor and Senior Associate Editor of the Papers of James Madison at the University of Virginia. He is the editor of several volumes of the Madison Papers and *James Madison's "Advice to My Country"* and the author of *Benjamin Lincoln and the American Revolution.*

Holly C. Shulman is Research Associate Professor in the Studies in Women and Gender program at the University of Virginia. She is the author of *The Voice of America: Propaganda and Democracy, 1942–1945,* co-editor of *The Encyclopedia of Eleanor Roosevelt,* and with David B. Mattern co-editor of *The Selected Letters of Dolley Payne Madison.* She is currently editing an electronic edition of the complete letters of Dolley Payne Madison.

Credits

Photo Credits

Editor Joanne Randolph

Series Design Laura Murawski

Layout Design Corinne Jacob

Photo Researcher Jeffrey Wendt